NO FRILLS Exam

Intellectual Properties, Trademarks and Copyrights

ExamREVIEW.NET (a.k.a. ExamREVIEW) is an independent content developer not associated/affiliated with the certification vendor(s) mentioned throughout this book. The name(s), title(s) and award(s) of the certification exam(s) mentioned in this book are the trademark(s) of the respective certification vendor(s). We mention these name(s) and/or the relevant terminologies only for describing the relevant exam process(es) and knowledge.

> We are NOT affiliated with the NHA. This book is also NOT endorsed by the NHA. NHA OWNS THE CEHRS TRADEMARK.

ExamREVIEW(TM) and ExamFOCUS(TM) are our own trademarks for publishing and marketing self-developed examprep books worldwide. The EXAMREVIEW.NET web site has been created on the Internet since January 2001. The EXAMFOCUS.NET division has its web presence established since 2009.

> Copyright 2015. ExamREVIEW.NET. All rights reserved.

Contents of this book are fully copyrighted. We develop study material entirely on our own. Braindump is strictly prohibited. We provide essential knowledge contents, NOT any generalized "study system" kind of "pick-the-right-answer-every time" techniques or "visit this link" referrals.

Contents Update

All books come with LIFE TIME FREE UPDATES. When you find a newer version of the purchased book all you need to do is to go and download. **Please check our web site's Free Updates section regularly:**

http://www.examreview.net/free_updates.htm

Page Formatting and Typeface

To accommodate the needs of those with weaker vision, we use LARGER PRINT throughout the book whenever practical. The text in this book was created using Garamond (size 16). A little bit of page resizing, however, may have happened along the actual book printing process.

The CEHRS Exam

The NHA Electronic Health Records Specialist Certification Exam aims at assessing the competencies of the Electronic Health Records Specialist. The exam tests the knowledge and abilities to effectively manage medical records in different healthcare settings.

The exam has multiple-choice items covering these topics:

- Demonstrate knowledge of the health care delivery system and medical terminology.

- Demonstrate an understanding of the transition to an Electronic Health Record (EHR).

- Demonstrate the ability to maintain an EHR within a physician's office.

- Demonstrate the ability to maintain an EHR within a hospital setting.

- Demonstrate an understanding of the usage of personal health records.

- Demonstrate knowledge of compliance and ethics.

- Demonstrate an understanding of the Practice Partner (the ambulatory EHR).

This book focuses on the technology topics of the exam. You should use this book together with other sources for comprehensive exam preparation.

Table of Contents (2015 Edition)

INTELLECTUAL PROPERTIES, TRADEMARKS AND COPYRIGHTS 1

CONTENTS UPDATE 2

PAGE FORMATTING AND TYPEFACE 2

THE CEHRS EXAM 2

HEALTH RECORD RETENTION 11
HEALTH DATABASE AND DATAWAREHOUSE 12
INFORMATION NEEDS AND DATA INTEGRITY 13
LOGICAL STRUCTURE 14
MASTER TABLE, VIEWS, KEYS AND INDEXES 15
IDENTIFIERS 16
THE ROLE OF HIM PROFESSIONAL 17
CLINICAL VOCABULARIES AND CLINICAL DATA REPRESENTATIONS 18
HEALTHCARE INFORMATICS AND DOCUMENTATION STANDARDS 20
JCAHO AND HIMSS 21
INTEGRATED CLINICAL SYSTEM 22
MEDICARE, MEDICAID AND TRICARE 23
LEVELS OF CARE 24
DEFINING EHR 25
DEFINING AMBULATORY EHR 26
EHR AND MEANINGFUL USE 27
AHR, EMR, CDR AND CPR 28
THE REGISTRATION PORTION OF AN EHR 29
EHR INTEROPERABILITY 30

EHR STANDARDS 31
HL7 32
CDA, CCD AND CCR 33
ONTOLOGY AND RADT 34
LIS 35
CDSS 36
LABORATORY INFORMATICS, HEALTH INFORMATICS AND LIMS 37
EPIDEMIOLOGY, PHARMACOEPIDEMIOLOGY, ETHNOPHARMACOLOGY, ETHNOBOTANY AND
PHARMACOVIGILANCE 38
RIS AND CDS 39
CPOE 40
ICD AND ITS REVISIONS 41
ICF 43
SNOMED 44
LOINC 45
PROBLEMS OF IMPLEMENTATION 46
INFORMATION FLOW AND CODING 47
ROLE OF A MEDICAL CODER 48
PATIENT MASTER INDEX 49
MAKING CHANGES TO THE EHR RECORDS 50
ROI OF EHR DEPLOYMENT 52
CLINICAL DATA ENTRY 53
POMR AND SOAP 54
MEDICAL RECORD DOCUMENTATION 55
HEALTH INFORMATION REVIEW 56
HEALTH INFORMATION MANAGEMENT 57
HEALTH INFORMATION QUALITY 58
HEALTH INFORMATION BACKUP 59
HEALTH INFORMATION LEVEL OF ACCESS AND UPDATE 60
HEALTH INFORMATION SECURITY AND PROTECTION 61
HEALTH INFORMATION PRIVACY AND THE HIPAA PRIVACY RULE 63
THE HIPAA SECURITY RULE 65
HIPPA RISK ASSESSMENT 66
INFORMATION DISPOSAL UNDER HIPPA 67
ONC, SHARP AND HITECH 68
THE AAA CONCEPT AND ACCESS CONTROL MEASURES 69
SECURITY CHECKLIST 72
SECURITY CHECKLIST SPECIFIC TO EHR 73
ESTABLISHING ACCOUNTABILITY THROUGH EVENT LOGGING 74
GETTING A LITTLE BIT TECHNICAL INTO COMPUTER SECURITY 75
DEFENSE IN DEPTH 77
SECURITY ASSUMPTIONS 78
MALWARE AND VIRUSES 79
SOFTWARE FLAWS 81
SNIFFING, EAVESDROPPING, FOOTPRINTING AND SOCIAL ENGINEERING 82
SECURITY MANAGEMENT ACTIVITIES 83
INFORMATION SECURITY STANDARDS 84
EHR UPGRADE 86
EHR CONTINUITY AND DISASTER RECOVERY 87
REVIEW QUESTIONS AND ANSWERS 90

Elements of a Health Record

Formally speaking, a health record is a written collection of information about a patient. Such a record is derived from the patient's first encounter or treatment at a hospital, clinic or other primary health care centre. It is thus a record of all the procedures carried out on that patient, whilst he is in hospital or under treatment at a clinic or centre. It should contain the past medical history of the patient, including opinions, investigations and other details relevant to the health of the patient.

An accurate and complete health record would be of great value to:

- the patient

- the institution (hospital, clinic, or other health facility)

- the doctor and other health professionals

- the researchers

- the billing department

Health records are kept initially for communication between persons responsible for the care of the patient for present and future needs. In a typical setting, the registration staff of the hospital would collect identification information and figure out the patient's financial status. While under care, people who may contribute to the health record may include:

- medical staff such as consultants, physicians, surgeons, obstetricians, etc

- nurses

- physical therapists

- occupational therapists

- medical social workers

- lab technicians

In the context of Medical-legal, the main use of the record is as evidence of unbiased opinion of a patient's condition, history and prognosis, all assessed at a time when there was no thought of court action, and therefore extremely valuable. It may be used both in and outside the court for settlement of disputes.

A health record must contain sufficient information to IDENTIFY the patient, SUPPORT the diagnosis, JUSTIFY the treatment, and DOCUMENT the results facts accurately. Only one health record should be kept for each patient.

In a source oriented medical record, the information about a patient's care and illness is typically organized according to the "source" of the information within the record, usually presented in chronological order. Structured records are more easily automated. A disadvantage is that there is less room for individual description and health workers find it too restricting.

Flow sheets provide the most appropriate method of monitoring a patient's progress. They are often used with source oriented health records. The steps necessary for designing a flow sheet include:

- defining the clinical setting within which the flow sheet will be used

- defining the clinical status of the patient to be monitored

- defining the monitoring frequency of data collection required to give maximum care

When dictating a problem oriented discharge summary, one can briefly summarize the therapeutic outcomes, which resulted in the resolution of a patient's specific problems. The logical display system used in the structured problem oriented health record would start with the database to collect information, followed by a problem list, which helps the doctor decide what is wrong with the patient. Such information is placed at the front of the record so everyone caring for the patient is aware of all problems. From the database and problem list, the initial plan for treatment and diagnostic work-up can be developed.

Progress notes may be narrative or in the form of a flow sheet. Generally, they should provide a pertinent chronological report of a patient's course in the health care facility and should reflect any change in condition as well as the result of treatment and the corresponding plan for future care. An admission progress note should summarize the present illness, pertinent past history, physical and laboratory findings, and the initial impressions of the physician and/or the initial diagnostic and therapeutic plan. An authenticated progress note should be prepared daily to document the medical necessity and acute level of care provided. Very importantly, all progress notes must be signed, dated and timed.

Consultation reports should also be included as part of the patient's medical record. They should show evidence of review by the consultant, any pertinent findings upon patient examination together with the consultant's opinion, recommendations and signature. The reason for the consultation should also be recorded. Also, an operative or other high-risk procedure report should be entered into the health record upon completion of any operative or high-risk procedure. If a full report cannot be entered immediately, at least a brief progress note should be entered.

Contents and Structure of a Health Record

When identifying and defining the general content and structure of the patient health record, one needs to establish the standard minimal components of all patient records and their content as required in all healthcare delivery environments. One must consider different views of the patient care record which might be required in each healthcare delivery setting. It would also be important to ensure that the contents in question can truly conform to the known health data standards. In any case, make sure the health record structure can enable a health care practitioner to:

- to identify the patient and provide care accordingly

- to determine the patient's condition at a specific point in time

- to review the diagnosis and therapeutic procedures that have been performed on the patient

- to render an opinion after examination

Very importantly, the record must enable another practitioner to assume patient care at any time!

Healthcare location and setting information is typically captured by using specific synopsis data sets pre-established for each setting. As a matter of fact, such data often serves as an index of an individual's pattern of healthcare.

Patient Charge Sheet

The charge sheet is an important document along the charge-capture process. Information found in a typical patient charge sheet may include and may not limit to:

- Attending Physician

- Referring Physician

- Admit Date & Date of Service

- Type & Place of Service

- Prior Authorization Number

- Modifiers

- Procedure code & Diagnosis Code

- Number Of days

- Location Details

- Physician Name, Address and Provider ID

You want to know that:

- The attending physician is the rendering physician who renders the service to the patient.

- The referring Physician is the physician who refers the patient to the attending physician.

- The Admit Date is the date in which patient was first admitted. The Date of Service was the date in which services were actually rendered.

- Preauthorization may be an insurance plan requirement in which the primary care physician must notify the insurance company in advance on certain medical procedures.

- Procedure codes are for indicating the kind of treatment or service that has been administered.

- A Charge Description Master CDM (AKA chargemaster) refers to a comprehensive listing of items that may be billable to a patient.

Health Record Retention

This is a policy concern rather than a technical one. Proper patient health record retention criteria for both written and electronic records must be established to conform to the requirements of Federal and state statutes. In fact, these criteria should specify retention according to the clinical value (the long-term and short-term clinical value) of data elements over time.

Traditionally, medical records were written on paper and kept in organized folders. Records that are considered active are housed at the clinical site, while older inactive records are kept in separate lower cost facilities.

In the US, state laws generally govern how long health records are to be kept. However, the HIPAA administrative simplification rules require a covered entity to keep documentation for 6 years. In fact, the HIPAA requirements will always preempt state laws in the case they mandate a shorter period.

Health Database and Datawarehouse

The most common form of database used in the healthcare industry is the relational database. In the context of relational database, the types of information saved are called 'entities', while those data elements that you want to save for each entity are being referred to as 'attributes'.

Attributes that can have only a single value at a time are being referred to as single-valued. A multi-valued attribute, in contrast, can have more than one value at one time. Composite attributes may be divided into smaller subparts as needed. Relationship is the connection between different entities, while cardinality is about how much of one side of the relationship belongs to how much of the other side. It may exist in four types, which are:

- one-to-one

- one-to-many

- many-to-one

- many-to-many

Between the different entities involved there may be a mutual dependency, meaning that one item cannot exist if the other item does not exist.

A data warehouse refers to a centrally managed yet easily accessible repository of data collected in the transaction information system. The data are usually aggregated, organized, catalogued and structured to facilitate read intensive search, queries, and analysis. The core idea of data warehousing is that the many disparate systems that held un-integrated data should get themselves properly integrated.

Information Needs and Data Integrity

Information needs of healthcare is rather unique. You should think in terms of the events that trigger the gathering of information - while a business transaction is repetitive and is usually dominated by numerical data, in healthcare you seldom see repetitive transaction activities.

Most of the time the "transaction" in healthcare is fairly unique. Also, since the recording of the interactions that take place between the patient and the care giver is rather verbiage, textual representation instead of numbers is the dominating data type involved.

Data integrity is the key to developing a quality health information database. Without accurate data, the users will lose confidence in the database. Data integrity is not easy to maintain but there are straightforward ways to enforce constraints to prevent problems from happening. The identification, interpretation, and application of rules for processing health information, however, may present a more challenging problem. This is especially true when rules must be communicated and translated and that much of the meaning and intent may get lost along this process.

Logical Structure

The logical design of the base data structures used for storing health data is highly important. The key is to properly arrange the data into a logical structure which can be mapped into the physical database design to satisfy the need of the users.

When defining the logical structure of the patient record, one should ensure consistency in the data organization and whenever possible promote the efficient transfer of data through adopting a common record transfer convention. Data consistency is a term that summarizes the validity, accuracy, usability and integrity of related data between different applications that are linked together.

One should specify data element definitions to conform to all the relevant standards. It would be particularly important to identify and reference appropriate coding systems consistent with current and future health reporting retrieval, analysis, and reimbursement needs.

Master Table, Views, Keys and Indexes

The foundation of every health database system is a database component called table. Every database has one or more tables for storing data. Typically, each database table is given its own unique name and consists of multiple columns and rows. Each database table column (a.k.a table fields) has its own unique name and pre-defined data type.

A view is different, it is simply a subset of the database sorted and displayed in a particular manner suitable for particular users. Simply put, a view is usually configured to display some or all of the database fields according to user requirements. In fact, views often use filters for determining which records to show.

A popular approach to defining EHR content is through master tables and data views. A master table has a list of variables that represent the range of attributes currently defined for a given subject. By using these master tables one can provide both a short term and long term approach to methodically addressing EHR content (and keeping the content under proper coordination and implementation). Master tables should be developed and refined as necessary. They should also provide the means of proposing minimum content by EHR areas. A primary key (PK) refers to one or more data attributes that uniquely identify an entity. A key that consists of two or more attributes is called a composite key. The various identifiers usually serve well as the primary keys. The Foreign Key (FK) is different - it is an entity that serves the reference to the primary key of another entity.

Database indexes make finding a piece of data easy. Instead of searching through each record in a database, a search can in fact be directed by an index to the appropriate data. Do note that the effective use of indexes would require establishing a proper balance between an efficient number of indexes and too many.

Identifiers

Identifiers are for uniquely identifying healthcare providers, healthcare organizations, and individuals who provide or seek healthcare services. These identifiers often serve as the keys in the health information databases.

In the US, the Social Security Number (SSN) is often being considered for use as the choice of patient identifier. However, there are concerns on the use of SSN for this purpose since:

- not everyone has an SSN;

- several individuals may share the use of the same SSN;

- SSN in fact presents an exposure to possible violations of confidentiality.

The Health Care Financing Administration (HCFA) has produced a popular provider identifier known as the Universal Physician Identifier Number (UPIN), which can only be assigned to those physicians who handle Medicare patients. The Health Industry Number (HIN) was issued by the Health Industry Business Communications Council (HIBCC) to serve as an identifier for healthcare facilities, practitioners, and retail pharmacies. HCFA had also produced another provider of service identifiers for Medicare usage. The Labeler Identification Code (LIC) is issued by HIBCC for identifying manufacturer and/or distributor. The Universal Product Code (UPC) is maintained by the Uniform Code Council for labeling those products sold in retail channels.

FYI, the ASTM E1714 - 07 provides a set of requirements outlining those properties that are required to create a universal healthcare identifier (UHID) system.

The role of HIM professional

Health record is the property of the hospital or clinic which serves as a medico legal document for the benefit of the patient, the doctor, and the hospital or clinic. Such health record should contain sufficient information to enable another doctor to take over the care of the patient if required, and for a consultant to give a satisfactory opinion when requested.

The responsibility for the accuracy and completeness of a health record rests with the attending doctor, while the health information management/health record professional is responsible to the hospital administrator for providing the necessary services to the medical staff to assist with the development and maintenance of a complete and accurate health record.

Clinical Vocabularies and Clinical Data Representations

Clinical Vocabularies play a strategic role in providing access to computerized health information since clinicians may use a variety of terms for the same concept. Standard vocabularies are a means of encoding data for exchange, comparison, or aggregation among systems.

When a clinician evaluates a patient, free text or unstructured information such as history and physical findings is first captured. As the clinician evaluation process continues, the unstructured data is transformed by a clinical coding specialist into more structured data that linked to payment processing and reimbursement. These are claims-related structured data sets that are different from clinical vocabularies. They include:

- Current Procedure Terminology (CPT) codes

- International Classification of Diseases (ICD)

- Diagnosis Related Groups (DRG)

These data sets are primarily used for structured billing only. On the other hand, clinical data representations are widely used to document diagnoses and procedures. Codes widely accepted in the US include:

- International Classification of Diseases (ICD) codes

- Current Procedural Terminology (CPT) codes

- Systematized Nomenclature of Human and Veterinary Medicine (SNOMED) codes

- Laboratory Observation Identifier Names and Codes (LOINC)

- Diagnostic and Statistical Manual of Mental Disorders (DSM) codes

- Diagnostic Related Groups (DRGs) codes

- National Drug Code (NDC)

- Gabrieli Medical Nomenclature (GMN) codes

- Unified Medical Language System (UMLS) codes

Healthcare Informatics and Documentation Standards

Formally speaking, health informatics refers to the discipline which is at the intersection of information science, computer science, and health care.

Healthcare standards in the US are produced by ACR/NEMA, ASC X12N, ASTM, HL7, IEEE, and NCPDP. Their activities are coordinated through the ANSI Healthcare Informatics Standards Planning Panel (HISPP).

Healthcare informatics and documentation standards are essential for a highly efficient EHR since information that is to be stored in the EHR will come from many different sources. Message standards must therefore be in place to ensure that data can be transmitted from a source system to an EHR without extensive human intervention. In fact, standard terminology, codes, and formats are seen as the key factors to the successful aggregation of different EHRs for research and other purposes.

JCAHO and HIMSS

The Joint Commission on the Accreditation of Healthcare Organizations (JCAHO) sets standards for healthcare organizations and issues accreditation to organizations that meet those standards. JCAHO standards address an organization's performance in key functional areas. Each standard is presented as a series of "Elements of Performance" (EP), which represents expectations that establish the broad framework that JCAHO surveyors use to evaluate a facility's performance.

JCAHO conducts periodic on-site surveys to verify that an accredited organization can substantially comply with Joint Commission standards and continuously makes efforts to improve the care and services it provides.

The Healthcare Information and Management Systems Society (HIMSS) is a membership organization which focuses on advocating the optimal use of healthcare information technology and management systems for the betterment of healthcare.

Integrated Clinical System

The reasons to move to an electronic system are plentiful:

- Improve the accuracy and quality of data recorded in a health record

- Enhance healthcare practitioners' access to a patient's healthcare information

- Improve the quality of care

- Improve the efficiency of the health record service

- Contain healthcare costs

The major value of an integrated clinical system is that it can enable the capture of clinical data as a part of the overall workflow. The use of standard clinical vocabularies and structured data organization (ontologies) can greatly enhance the ability of clinical systems to interoperate meaningfully.

Medicare, Medicaid and Tricare

Medicare is a US based health insurance program for people age 65 or older; people under age 65 with certain disabilities, and people of all ages with End-Stage Renal Disease. When we say "people" we mean people in the US.

Medicare is a Federal health insurance program. It pays for hospital and medical care for the elderly (and also certain disabled Americans). It has two main parts for hospital and medical insurance (which are Part A and Part B) as well as two additional parts for flexibility and prescription drugs (which are Part C and Part D). Medicaid is a means-tested health and medical services program. It is for certain individuals and families with low incomes. Although primary oversight is handled at the federal level, each state can establish its own eligibility standards.

You want to know that Medicare systems use extensive Personally Identifiable Information on beneficiaries. Electronic Data Interchange can take place only when providers can have access to Medicare Systems, but the information involved as well as the purposes of use are limited to protect beneficiaries. In fact each healthcare provider must first complete an EDI Enrollment form prior to starting to exchange data with Medicare.

TRICARE is formerly known as the Civilian Health and Medical Program of the Uniformed Services (CHAMPUS). It is a health care program of the Department of Defense Military Health System which provides civilian health benefits for military personnel, military retirees, and their dependents. It is managed by TRICARE Management Activity (TMA) and is under the authority of the Assistant Secretary of Defense.

Levels of Care

Primary care describes the health services by those healthcare providers who server as the principal point of consultation for patients. Secondary care refers to services provided by medical specialists who do not have first contact with patients.

In many cases, patients are required to first see a primary care provider for referral before accessing secondary care. In fact, this kind of restriction is often found under the terms of the payment agreements in health insurance plans.

Tertiary care refers to specialized consultative health care in facility that has personnel and equipments for advanced medical investigation and treatment. Quaternary care is an extension of tertiary care in reference to highly specialized medicine of an advanced level. The services involved are usually only offered in a limited number of health care centers.

Defining EHR

Electronic Health Record (EHR) is not a simple replacement of the paper record. It is a longitudinal electronic record of patient health information generated by one or more encounters in any care delivery setting. Simply put, an EHR integrates data to serve different needs. The purpose is to collect data once, then use it multiple times. The EHR can generate a complete record of a clinical patient encounter, as well as supporting other care-related activities directly or indirectly via interface.

Do note that even though EHR should reflect the entire health history of an individual across his or her lifetime including data from multiple providers from a variety of healthcare settings, practically it is most often generated and maintained within an institution and is not yet a truly longitudinal record of all care provided to the patient in all venues over time. Examples of item to be included as part of the history includes:

- the present illness

- the immunization status

- any relevant past, family, and social histories

- the use of any preexisting medical devices

- any special consideration of daily activities

- any family expectation for and/or involvement in the assessment, treatment, and continuous care of the patient

FYI, the ASTM Standard E1384 outlines practice for Content and Structure of the EHR.

Defining Ambulatory EHR

Ambulatory EHR is a specific kind of digital medical record intended to be easily transported.

The EHR behind a typical hospital environment (Inpatient EHR) is quite different from that of an ambulatory environment.

Even though a hospital is not a single system but a collection of systems within various departments, thing are mostly locally housed. In an ambulatory environment, there is a need for records to be portable and accessible from anywhere since referrals to and from outside stand-alone practices are significant.

Ambulatory EHR is not necessarily good for a typical inpatient setting. For example, an ambulatory EHR has to be capable of electronic prescribing to the outside pharmacies while there is no such need for an inpatient system.

EHR and meaningful use

According to the American Recovery and Reinvestment Act of 2009, "Meaningful" Use requires:

- the use of a certified EHR in a meaningful manner, such as e-prescribing.

- the use of certified EHR technology for electronic exchange of health information to improve quality of health care.

- the use of certified EHR technology to submit clinical quality and other measures.

To demonstrate meaningful use successfully, one must be able to report clinical quality measures. There are different objectives for eligible professionals and hospitals.

AHR, EMR, CDR and CPR

Other similar terms include Automated Health Records (AHR), Electronic Medical Record (EMR), and Computer-based Patient Record (CPR). The term AHR has been used to describe a collection of computer-stored images of traditional health record documents. Typically, these documents are scanned into a computer and the images are stored on optical disks.

The term EMR, as with Automated Health Records, has been used to describe automated systems based on document imaging or systems which have been developed within a medical practice or community health centre. These have been used extensively by general practitioners in many developed countries and include patient identification details, medications and prescription generation, laboratory results and in some cases all healthcare information recorded by the doctor during each visit by the patient.

EMRs are computerized legal clinical records, while EHRs represent the ability to share medical information among stakeholders, including consumers, healthcare providers, employers and the government. Before effective EHRs can be made possible, the provider organizations must first implement complete EMR systems. Clinical data repository (CDR) is a real-time transaction-processing database of all clinical patient information. The CDR is typically fed from ancillary systems such as laboratory, radiology, and pharmacy as well as displays, among other clinical and administrative data and current results of tests and procedures to the caregivers.

In the US the term CPR was introduced in the 1990's. This was defined as a collection of health information for one patient linked by a patient identifier. The CPR could include as little as a single episode of care for a patient or healthcare information over an extended period of time.

The Registration Portion of an EHR

The registration portion of an EHR contains a unique patient identifier consisting of a numeric or alphanumeric sequence that is unidentifiable outside the organization or institution in which it serves. This unique patient identifier is sometimes referred to as the medical record number or master patient index (MPI), which is the core of an EHR and links all clinical observations, tests, procedures, complaints, evaluations, and diagnoses to the patient.

All patients should be registered into an established EHR system - this should be done by capturing the demographic information that can sufficiently identify the patient for the purpose of opening a formal patient record. The goal of obtaining this information is to allow the repeated and accurate identification of patients from one care setting in another, so to provide a link for collecting additional healthcare information over time.

EHR Interoperability

Electronic clinical documentation systems can enhance the value of EHRs through providing electronic capture of clinical notes; patient assessments; and clinical reports, such as medication administration records (MAR).

To create interoperable EHRs, standards would be needed for clinical vocabularies, for healthcare message exchanges, and for EHR ontologies. Additionally, EHR systems must follow appropriate privacy and security standards related to the HIPAA regulations.

EHR standards

The main organizations that create standards related to EHRs include Health Level Seven (HL7), Comite Europeen de Normalization – Technical Committee (CEN TC) 215, and the American Society for Testing and Materials (ASTM) E31.

HL7 operates in the US for developing the most widely used healthcare-related electronic data exchange standards in North America. CEN TC 215, on the other hand, is the preeminent healthcare IT standards developing organization in Europe. Both HL7 and CEN promptly collaborate with the ASTM.

Guidelines and standards for the content and structure of computer patient record systems are being dealt with by the ASTM Subcommittees E31.12 and E31.19.

The "Standard Description for Content and Structure of the Computer-based Patient Record" has been made within Subcommittee E31.19. (ASTM, 1994), which includes work from HISPP on data modeling and an expanded framework that includes master tables and also data views by user.

HL7

Health Level 7 (HL7) is a messaging standard widely used in messaging across health care applications. It is being used for sending structured, encoded, data from one application (such as the laboratory system) to another (such as the EHR). There are two major versions of HL7 (v2.x and v3.0) in use today.

HL7 v. 2x is commonly used by existing Commercial-off-the shelf (COTS) applications. HL7 v. 3 is the Reference Information Model (RIM) which provides a much more robust ability to represent complex relationships. Note that the HL7 v3 standard is based on a formal methodology known as the HDF. It also works following object-oriented principles.

HDF (HL7 Version 3 Development Framework) is a continuously evolving process which aims to develop specifications for facilitating interoperability between different healthcare systems.

CDA, CCD and CCR

The HL7 Clinical Document Architecture CDA is a XML-based markup standard. It aims to specify the encoding, structure and semantics of exchanging clinical documents. With it, a clinical document has a number of characteristics, including Persistence; Stewardship; Potential for authentication; Context; Wholeness and Human readability.

This standard serves as the basis for the Continuity of Care Document CCD specification in the US. On the other hand, Continuity of Care Record CCR is a health record standard specification aims to facilitate sharing of records, and is jointly developed by ASTM International, the Massachusetts Medical Society (MMS), the Healthcare Information and Management Systems Society (HIMSS), the American Academy of Family Physicians (AAFP), the American Academy of Pediatrics (AAP) and others. With it, there are 6 sections that must be included in the record, which are Header, Patient Identifying Information, Patient Financial and Insurance Information, Health Status of the Patient, Care Documentation, and Care Plan Recommendation.

CCR uses XML, therefore a CCR can be created, read, and interpreted by any EHR software. Extensible Markup Language XML is a general-purpose markup language which is "extensible" as it allows users to define their own tags. With XML different commercial systems may communicate so that the exchange of information can become much easier.

Ontology and RADT

An ontology refers to the specification of a representational vocabulary for a shared domain of discourse, including definitions of classes, relations, functions, and other objects…etc. Simply put, ontologies are used by people, databases, and applications that need to share domain information. They are typically structured in such a way as to have computer-usable definitions of basic concepts in the domain together with their relationships.

Different ontologies may model the same concepts in different ways. In order for systems to be able to integrate information into different ontologies, there need to be primitives (in other words the core relationships and definitions) for different ontologies to map terms to their equivalents in other ontologies.

Registration, admissions, discharge, and transfer (RADT) OR Admissions, Discharge, Transfer/Registration (ADT/R) data are the key components of EHRs. These data include vital information for accurate patient identification and assessment, such as name, demographics, next of kin, employer information, chief complaint, patient disposition, etc. Such data allows an individual's health information to be aggregated for use in clinical analysis and research.

LIS

Laboratory information systems (LIS) are used as hubs to integrate orders, results from laboratory instruments, schedules, billing, and other administrative information. HOWEVER, laboratory data is integrated entirely with the EHR only infrequently. In fact, a majority of LIS installations are standalone - not integrated with EHRs.

At a minimum, a LIS should provide these features or functionalities:

- Patient Check In

- Order Entry

- Specimen Processing

- Result Entry and Reporting

- Patient and Physician Demographics

CDSS

Clinical decision support system (CDSS) is a special kind of interactive decision support system that can assist health professionals with their decision making tasks by linking health observations with health knowledge to influence the health choices made.

The two main types of CDSS are Knowledge-Based and Non-Knowledge-Based. The former has three parts, which are the knowledge base, inference engine, and mechanism to communicate. The knowledge base has rules and associations in the form of IF-THEN rules. The inference engine is responsible for combining rules with actual patient's data. The communication mechanism presents the results to the users.

CDSS with a non-Knowledge-Based nature makes use of artificial intelligence and machine learning to learn from past experiences through finding patterns in clinical data. Examples include artificial neural networks and genetic algorithms.

Laboratory Informatics, Health Informatics and LIMS

Laboratory Informatics refers to the specialized application of information technology for optimizing laboratory operations. It typically encompasses a number of elements, such as electronic lab notebooks, sample management, data acquisition, data processing, reporting and scientific data management.

The term Health informatics describes a discipline which is at the intersection of information science, computer science, and health care. It has to deal with a number of things, including resources, devices, and methods required to optimize the acquisition, storage, retrieval, and use of health information.

Laboratory information management system LIMS has the core function of managing samples. It tracks the entire chain of custody and sample location. It also offers close integration with modern laboratory instruments and applications.

Epidemiology, Pharmacoepidemiology, Ethnopharmacology, Ethnobotany and Pharmacovigilance

Epidemiology is all about the study of human health in populations. It looks into the causes of illness, how a disease may get spread, as well as disease control.

Pharmacoepidemiology combines aspects of pharmacology and epidemiology for examining patterns of drug usage among large populations.

Ethnopharmacology involves studying ethnic groups and their health, how their health relates to their lifestyle as well as their ways and patterns of using medicines.

Ethnobotany refers to the study of how different cultures use medicinal plants.

Pharmacovigilance deals with the tracking of medications in the market for their side effects and other problems.

RIS and CDS

Radiology information systems (RIS) are typically used by radiology departments to tie together patient radiology data and images.

A typical RIS would include patient tracking, scheduling, results reporting, and image tracking functions. Note that RIS systems are usually used in conjunction with picture archiving communications systems (PACS) for managing digital radiography studies.

Chromatography data system (CDS) refers to the software one can use to collect and analyze chromatographic results delivered by chromatography detectors.

CPOE

Computerized physician order entry (CPOE) can permit clinical providers to electronically order laboratory, pharmacy, and radiology services. These systems offer a range of functionality, from pharmacy ordering capabilities alone to more sophisticated systems such as complete ancillary service ordering, alerting, customized order sets, and result reporting. Do note that CPOE cannot entirely eliminate error. In fact it may introduce new types of error.

Previous studies had yielded evidence that medication error rate and errors that have potential for serious harm or death can be significantly reduced. HOWEVER, there are drawbacks and limitations. CPOE systems can take years to implement. Staff inexperience can cause slower entry of orders. Automation can also cause a false sense of security.

ICD and its revisions

The International Classification of Disease (ICD) is published by the World Health Organization (WHO). The ICD CM (Clinical Modification) is developed by the National Center for Health Statistics for use in the US, with the purpose of coding and classifying morbidity data from the inpatient and outpatient records, physician offices, and most National Center for Health Statistics surveys.

As said by the CDC, the IDC provides a format for reporting causes of death on the death certificate. The reported conditions are translated into medical codes following some coding rules, thus improving the usefulness of mortality statistics in these ways:

- giving preference to categories

- consolidating conditions

- systematically selecting a single cause of death from a reported sequence of conditions

There have been 10 revisions of the ICD so far:

1st Rev 1900-09

2d Rev 1910-20

3d Rev 1921-29

4th Rev 1930-38

5th Rev 1939-48

6th Rev 1949-57

7th Rev 1958-67

8th Rev 1968-78

9th Rev 1979-98

10th Rev 1999-present

As of the time of this writing, the 2015 version is available via:

http://apps.who.int/classifications/icd10/browse/2015/en

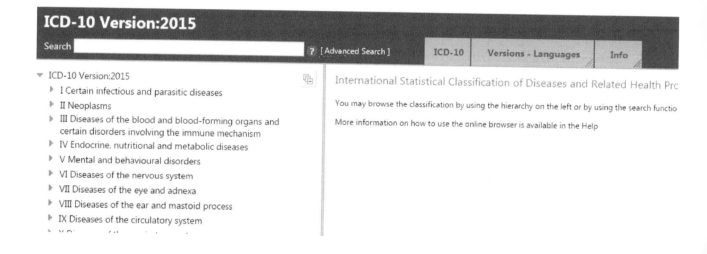

ICF

The ICF (International Classification of Functioning, Disability and Health) classification is in a position to complement the ICD-10. It is structured around:

- Body functions and structure

- Activities and participation

- Other information on severity and environmental factors

The language of the ICF is said to be made neutral as to etiology, thus placing the emphasis on function, NOT condition or disease. You can browse the ICF core set via: http://www.icf-core-sets.org/en/page1.php

Creation of an ICF Based Documentation Form

Selection Process - Step 1

Please select one (or more) ICF Core Set(s)

To select more than one ICF Core Set mark the ICF Core Sets by holding the CTRL-button pressed.

Generic Set
Disability Set

MUSCULOSKELETAL ICF CORE SETS:
Musculoskeletal Acute Comprehensive
Musculoskeletal Acute Brief
Musculoskeletal Post-Acute Comprehensive

SNOMED

Systematized Nomenclature of Medicine (SNOMED) is developed by SNOMED International which is a division of the College of American Pathologists (CAP). It is designed to be a comprehensive, multi-axial, controlled terminology, created for the indexing of the entire medical record. Its new version is called SNOMED-RT (Reference Terminology).

SNOMED-CT (Clinical Terms) aims at specifying the core file structure of SNOMED Clinical Terms. It is a new collaborative terminology being developed jointly by the National Health Service in the United Kingdom and the CAP, for integrating the British system of Read Codes and SNOMED-RT.

The relevant concept uses some axes that comprise terms formally organized in the format of hierarchical tree. These axes include (and not limit to):

- T (Topography)

- M (Morphology)

- L (Living organisms)

- C (Chemical)

- F (Function)

- J (Occupation)

- D (Diagnosis)

- P (Procedure)

- G (General)

LOINC

Logical Observation Identifiers, Names, and Codes (LOINC) codes are used for identifying individual laboratory results, clinical observations, and diagnostic study observations in laboratory systems. In fact it is one of the standards being used in the US Federal Government systems for the electronic exchange of clinical health information.

A unique 6-part name is given to each term for observation identity. Each database record has 6 fields for use as part of a unique specification of the observations. The fields are:

- Component

- Kind of property

- Time aspect

- System

- Type of scale

- Type of method

Problems of Implementation

In many areas, costs, available technology, lack of technical expertise and computer skills of staff, and lack of data processing facilities are in fact major issues which would need to be addressed before implementation of EHR is possible. Also, resistance by some medical practitioners and health professionals generally to a change from manual to electronic documentation may be a problem as well. You want to know that these problems as well as privacy and confidentiality issues must be addressed and quality control measures introduced before a successful change can be implemented.

Whether a manual or electronic health record is maintained there is the pressing need for ensuring that the information generated by healthcare providers is accurate, timely, and available when needed. Also, there is a need to ensure information can be exchanged between different systems. Health information exchange HIE focuses on the mobilization of healthcare information electronically across organizations that use disparate health care information systems.

Successful implementation of an EHR will ALWAYS be dependent on the computer skills of all healthcare professionals and other staff.

Information Flow and Coding

Even though the introduction of an EHR is aimed at increasing the efficiency of healthcare delivery by the institution and/or country, and containing costs by eliminating the unnecessary duplication of services, most of the time information flow for inpatients should be the same as for manual medical records.

Accurate classification of diseases treated and procedures performed is a major part of the work of the health record services. However, it is always not performed accurately or in a timely fashion due to problems such as poorly documented and incomplete medical records, lack of standard terminology, and poorly trained coding staff.

Computer-assisted coding requires that staff be well trained in coding and health records need to be accurate and complete. Standard terminology should also be imbedded in the system. Do note that the more structured the data coding demanded by the EHR system, the more knowledge and discipline would be required from the provider entering the data, and the more efforts within the organization would be required for managing the structure and code vocabulary/nomenclature being used.

Role of a Medical Coder

Medical coding refers to the process of transforming narrative descriptions of diseases, injuries, and healthcare procedures into numeric or alphanumeric designations in the form of code numbers. A medical coding specialist needs to read and review medical documentation provided by health care providers so to obtain detailed patient information including disease, injuries, surgical operations, and other procedures. This detailed information has to be translated into numeric codes using universally recognized coding systems. The code numbers are assigned to accurately describe the diagnoses as well as the procedures performed to examine the diagnoses.

The key is for the coding process to insure correct code selection for compliance with federal regulation and insurance requirements. Because the medical codes will be used extensively for reimbursement of hospital and physician claims, insurance and insurance fraud are the difficult topics that must be thoroughly understood.

Patient Master Index

A PMI is an index of all patients who have attended the hospital as an inpatient, outpatient or accident or emergency patient. It should only contain identifying and demographic information to be able to identify a patient's medical/health record. It should include the patient's full name, hospital medical record number, address, date of birth and age, national ID number (if any) or other piece of information that will help to uniquely identify that patient.

Making Changes to the EHR records

EHRs may not provide an easy distinction between original and edited text. The edited text can often occur with little or no versioning or track-changes functionality.

An addendum is new documentation used to add information to an original entry. They should be timely and should bear the current date and reason for the additional information being added to the health record. An organization must have a specific policy and procedure addressing how addendums are made in the health record. In addition, the organization should clearly define what type of information is considered an addendum.

An amendment is sort of a documentation meant to clarify health information within a health record. It is usually made after the original documentation has been completed by the provider. Keep in mind, amendments should be timely and bear the current date of documentation. An organization must have a procedure in place that specifies how this process will be completed so that the integrity of the record remains intact and in compliance with documentation standards. Note that some organizations may choose to implement policies and procedures that do not allow amendments. In such case, clarification would require the use of an addendum.

A correction is a change in the information meant to clarify inaccuracies after the original electronic document has been signed or rendered complete. Generally, there are quite many different ways to enter a correction within the EHR, and it may depend on the specific system the organization is implementing. An organization should have a clear policy and procedure regarding its system 's abilities regarding corrections. In addition, it should clearly define who can — unlock ‖ a document once it has been signed. Only one individual or department should have the ability to unlock a report, and the functionality should be carefully monitored and audited.

A deletion is the act of eliminating information from previously closed documentation without substituting new information. It is generally recommended that total elimination of information be disallowed. If an organization allows information to be deleted, it should require clear policies and procedures to ensure the integrity of the health record. A retraction, on the other hand, is the act of correcting information that was incorrect, invalid or made in error, by preventing display or hiding the entry or documentation from future general views. They are different from corrections in that they change the main point of the original documentation. Depending on the organization's electronic system, locked reports would usually require specific interventions for retracting information. Retractions should be made in the source system or where the documentation was originally created, as well as in any long term medical record or data repository system.

A late entry should only apply to documentation within the EHR that is entered after the point of care.

ROI of EHR Deployment

The definition of hard return on investment on EHRs generally involves two measurements, which are the quantifiable returns that can be demonstrated in financial terms and the process improvements that would suggest cost savings that may fit a measurable metric.

In general, hard ROI from EHR installations may be grouped into the major categories of patient flow, materials and staffing reductions, and billing improvements.

Clinical Data Entry

Use of local terminology can become a problem when trying to implement a system across a wide variety of healthcare settings or even within an institution. A data dictionary is a set of common standards for data collection and is used to promote uniformity in documentation, data processing and maintenance.

Clinical data standards may be developed to ensure that data collected in one hospital department or facility means the same in another department or facility. An institution may compile a simple data dictionary to meet the needs of their institution. Each entry in a data dictionary would contain data element such as 'personal identification' with a definition or descriptor such as "the unique number assigned to each patient within a hospital..." etc.

POMR and SOAP

The design of the POMR (Problem-Oriented Medical Record) is relevant to any electronic form of medical record. Its basic assumption is that medical care consists of four recurring phases of action, which are data collection, problem identification, planning, and follow-up.

The POMR format has four components, which correspond to four problem-solving steps: a database, problem list, plans and progress notes for each problem. Such structure is problem-oriented in two interrelated ways: (A) data in the record are labeled by the patient problem to which the data relate, and (B) problems are defined based on supporting data and patient needs, not provider hypotheses and purposes.

The Data Base section includes information such as patient's identification data, social and family history, immunizations and allergies. The Problem List section contains a list of patient's past and current problems. Each problem is assigned a unique number for future reference. The Management Plans section contains an up-to-date summary of each problem and management decisions. Diagnostic test results, medication and referral reports are generally summarized here as well. Note that each consultation is identified by its date of consultation, and that each problem managed during that consultation is recorded according to the problem number defined in the problem list.

The Subjective, Objective, Assessment, and Plan (aka S.O.A.P.) format is used as a guide for thorough recording of findings and decisions.

Medical Record Documentation

Inadequate medical record documentation is a major source of problem. Issues can include incomplete, insufficient or poor documentation and non-use of standard terminology. You must understand that a move to an electronic health record will not be successful if documentation deficiencies are not addressed and healthcare practitioners educated in good healthcare documentation. Health practitioners must always enter all relevant data at the point of care at the time that care is given.

Health Information Review

Prior to implementing electronic records, you want to first perform a review of the current Health Record System. Patient identification is a key issue in health information management as it is vital that each patient is uniquely identified. A well designed electronic health record really depends on the patient being correctly identified and all information for that patient maintained in the one record within the system.

Computerization and automation have had a marked effect on the production of morbidity statistics but if the original information is incorrect the statistics compiled will never be accurate. In fact one frequent problem which may need to be addressed prior to implementing an EHR is the lack of training of clerical staff on the need to carefully question each patient or relative to ensure that they can uniquely identify the patient. Incorrect spelling of names is always a problem when the clerical staff is not properly trained.

To identify a person you need to determine what piece of information is not likely to be changed. Names and addresses should not be used as they can be readily changed. Date of Birth could be used but it has been found that many people as they age cannot remember their birth date accurately.

Also keep in mind, a unique patient identification number is not the same as a hospital/medical record number. It is the means of uniquely identifying an individual – once identified, a hospital or medical record number is usually issued to enable all information on an individual patient to be filed and maintained within the one medical record.

Health Information Management

A standard form of consent should never replace a detailed and meaningful discussion with the client. Instead, it should simply be used as a method of documenting the fact that the discussion took place. A client may have the right to withhold their consent to having their health information maintained on an electronic system or transmitted via the Internet.

Reasonable expectations of the client are relevant when consent is obtained. One such expectation is that electronic health information will not be collected indiscriminately or stored unnecessarily. The principle for collecting, using and disclosing health information is that only the amount of health information that is essential for carrying out intended purpose should be collected, used or disclosed.

Once an electronic health information system is in place, the primary concern would be the integrity of the electronic health information and the safeguarding against potential corruption, unauthorized access and inadvertent purging.

Health Information Quality

According to Martin, (1976) qualities that computer-based information should possess should include:

- Accurate

- Tailored to the needs of the user

- Relevant

- Timely

- Immediately understandable

- Recognizable

- Attractively presented

- Brief

- Up-to-date

- Trustworthy

- Complete

- Easily accessible

Health Information Backup

It is imperative to routinely backup electronic health information to ensure that valuable information is not lost. Policy pertaining to data backup should include:

- Name of backup coordinator and record keeper;

- Method(s) used for data backups, with a checklist of procedures;

- Frequency of data backups;

- Location of on-site data storage;

- Location of off-site data storage; and

- Types of data (generally) to be backed up.

It is best practice to backup all electronic health information that is stored on the system's hard drive. Additionally, consideration should be made to the technical requirements for reading data backup files in the longer term. Keep in mind, marking data simply means that the database management system can overwrite the electronic health information if further space is required.

Health Information Level of Access and Update

Level of access should correspond with the confidential nature of the health information. There should be explicit organizational policies that address issues including but not limited to data access, audits and, security clearance. Access to electronic health information via computer terminal must be controlled through a protected, individual password and also through physical security measures. Computer terminals should not be left unattended if a user has logged in. Identity should be authenticated through a unique token. Each individual must be responsible for his or her own password and a policy should be implemented which requires the password to be changed routinely. All unauthorized accesses or attempts to access electronic health information should form part of an audit record that can be reviewed and provide evidence of violations or system misuse.

The electronic record system must be kept current by updating the hardware, software and conducting maintenance reviews. Security features must also be assessed on a regular basis.

Health Information Security and Protection

You want to know that:

- ASTM Subcommittee E31.12 on Computer-based Patient Records develops "Guidelines for Minimal Data Security Measures for the Protection of Computer-based Patient Records."

- ASTM Subcommittee E31.17 on Access, Privacy, and Confidentiality of Medical Records develops standards to address these issues.

- ASTM Subcommittee E31.20 develops standard specifications for electronic authentication of health information.

- The American Association for Medical Transcription (AAMT) prepares guidelines on confidentiality, privacy, and security of patient care documentation through the process of medical dictation and transcription.

Generally speaking, everyone involved (including the patient, healthcare professional and the general population) needs reassurance that all data generated is maintained in a secure environment. If an electronic record system is connected to the Internet firewall protection must be considered.

A firewall is blocking a computer's doorway to the Internet. Such protection can extend to both incoming and outgoing net traffic and nothing can bypass the firewall unless expressly permitted by the physiotherapist. A packet consists of a header which marks the beginning of the packet, a payload of data, and a trailer which marks the end of the packet. The checksum if available for error checking is located at the trailer. The header has to specify the data type in transit. A screened host gateway is a packet-filtering device which is configured to communicate only with a designated application gateway inside the protected network. It is designed to be very specific and highly restrictive in that no other traffic is ever allowed to go in and out of it.

A firewall prevents unauthorized access to or from a private network by examining each message and/or packet that passes through it and blocks those that do not meet the specified security criteria. Simply put, a firewall uses more sophisticated mechanisms (which are more dynamic in nature). The problem with firewalls is that they are generally not configured to offer protection from insider threats. In fact, protecting against insider threat will require different solutions.

If a wireless network or a virtual private network (VPN) is in use then the electronic health information must be encrypted. Encryption is the conversion of electronic health information into a form, called a ciphertext, which cannot be easily understood by unauthorized people. PPTP is a VPN protocol for older software based Windows clients (pre-Windows 2000). L2TP is a VPN protocol for newer software based Windows clients. IPSec is the standard protocol for hardware based VPN solutions. Making a VPN connection over an unsecured wireless network can be dangerous since it is technically possible for an attacker to hijack the connection. To add more security to the VPN connection you should implement certificates accordingly.

The primary concern with transmitting electronic health information is the inappropriate accessing of this information by third parties. The basic tenet of health information disclosure is that one should only disclose the absolute minimum health information required to fulfill the stated purpose. In an attempt to ensure that the recipient of electronic health information is in compliance with the standards established a transmission agreement should be in place. A sound transmission agreement can ensure that the recipient of electronic health information institute and adhere to the policies in place and provide one with indemnification should a breach of confidentiality occur.

Health Information Privacy and the HIPAA Privacy Rule

In general, research use of patient data drawn from the EHR should be provided as aggregate and unidentified data. Any research projects that seek the use of identified patient data should be reviewed and that such release must conform to the existing patient data confidentiality and security guidelines.

The HIPAA Privacy Rule's right of an individual to access protected health information (PHI) must be properly understood. This Privacy Rule serves to establish, with limited exceptions, an enforceable means by which individuals have a right to review or obtain copies of their PHI, to the extent it is maintained in the designated record set(s) of a covered entity. The Privacy Rule's specific, yet flexible, standards also address individuals' requests for access and timely action by the covered entity, including the provision of access, denial of access, and documentation.

Keep in mind, the Privacy Rule considers electronic documents to qualify as formal traditional written documents. Electronic information is being referred to as e-PHI.

The definition of a covered entity includes health plan, health care clearinghouse, and health care provider. A business associate is also covered under the rules. It refers to a person or entity that performs certain functions or activities that involve the use or disclosure of protected health information on behalf of, or provides services to, the covered entity.

The Privacy Rule requires covered entities to respond to requests for access in a timely manner. Unless otherwise stated, the Privacy Rule requires the individual be notified of the decision within 30 days of the covered entity's receipt of the request.

While the Privacy Rule's right of access belongs primarily to the individual who is the subject of the PHI, the Privacy Rule also generally requires that persons who are legally authorized to act on behalf of the individual regarding health care matters be granted the same right of access.

Note that the Privacy Rule would defer to state law to determine when a person has the legal authority to act on behalf of an individual with regard to health care matters. it does require covered entities to develop and implement reasonable policies and procedures to verify the identity of any person who requests PHI, as well as the authority of the person to have access to the information, if the identity or authority of the person is not already known.

Verification may be obtained either orally, or in writing (which may be satisfied electronically), so long as the requisite documentation, statements or representations are obtained where required by a specific Privacy Rule disclosure provision, and that the appropriate steps are ultimately taken to verify the identity and authority of individuals or personal representatives who are otherwise unknown.

The HIPAA Security Rule

The Security Standards for the Protection of Electronic Protected Health Information are collectively known as the Security Rule. The Security Rule is located at 45 CFR Part 160 and Subparts A and C of Part 164. It establishes a national set of security standards for protecting certain health information in electronic form. It applies to health plans, health care clearinghouses, and any health care provider who needs to transmit health information in electronic format (they call it e-PHI).

With the rule, a covered entity has to maintain administrative, technical, and physical safeguards for information protection so to ensure the confidentiality, integrity, and availability of electronic health information. Confidentiality means that e-PHI should not be made available or disclosed to unauthorized persons. Integrity means that e-PHI should not be altered or destroyed in any unauthorized way. Availability means that e-PHI should be made accessible and usable on demand by authorized users. Very importantly, one has to periodically review and update documentation in response to environmental or organizational changes that can affect the security of e-PHI.

Talking about Administrative Safeguards, one should identify and analyze potential risks to e-PHI and accordingly implement security measures. One should also designate a security official to develop and implement the relevant security policies and procedures. Information Access Management means authorizing access to e-PHI only when access is appropriate. Workforce Training and Management means training workforce members and applying sanctions against those workforce members who violate policies and procedures. Physical Safeguards include Facility Access and Control as well as Workstation and Device Security. Technical Safeguards include different forms of Access Control, Audit Controls, Integrity Controls and Transmission Security.

HIPPA Risk Assessment

The Security Rule requires a covered entity to perform risk analysis. A risk analysis process should be ongoing. It should involve evaluating the likelihood and impact of potential risks to e-PHI; implementing security measures to address the risks identified; documenting the chosen security measures; and maintaining continuous yet appropriate security protections.

Information disposal under HIPPA

Reasonable safeguards must be implemented to avoid prohibited, uses and disclosures of PHI. This includes the disposal of information. There should be procedures in place addressing the removal of electronic PHI from electronic media before disposing the media or making available the media available for re-use.

Depositing PHI/e-PHI in locked dumpsters that are accessible only by authorized persons is a viable option. Otherwise, clearing (via software or hardware that overwrites media with non-sensitive data), purging (via degaussing) or destroying the media (via disintegration, pulverization, melting, shredding...etc) should be considered.

Dumpster diving is about searching through the trash for confidential information. It is generally legal in the US except in some local jurisdictions.

ONC, SHARP and HITECH

The Health Information Technology for Economic and Clinical Health (HITECH) Act has been put in place with the goal of improving American health care delivery and patient care through making massive investment in health information technology. The Office of the National Coordinator for Health Information Technology (ONC) is in a position to coordinate programs for implementing HITECH.

Strategic Health IT Advanced Research Projects (SHARP) is a program led by several major universities for conducting breakthrough research to achieve tangible goals in different research areas over a four-year period. Results of the research will be translated into patient-centered health IT products and services.

The AAA concept and access control measures

The three "As" are often being referred to as the AAA concept. The general types of authentication are:

- Something a person knows (eg. password)
- Something a person has (eg. ID card)
- Something a person is (eg. role and title)

Strong authentication requires two of the above and is known as two-factor authentication. In fact, a major portion of what is required to address nonrepudiation is accomplished through the use of strong methods for authentication and ensuring data integrity. You should also consider to establish written standard business practices for creating a presumption of efficient and reliable operations.

Authorization determines if you can carry out the requested actions. Access criteria types include and not limited to:

- Roles
- Groups
- Physical or logical location
- Time of day
- Transaction type
- … etc

A common practice is to have all access criteria default to "no access" at the very beginning.

Below shows a list of recommended measures:

→ Users of the application should be identified (by a UserID), authenticated (by a password or token ...etc) and authorized (allowing the use of functionality required to perform their role).

→ System administrators should be subject to strong authentication such as fingerprints, iris scans, challenge/response devices featuring one-time passwords or smartcards. Personal Identification Numbers (PINs) and passwords can be combined with smart cards or biometrics for additional levels of authentication. The proper use of PIN for authentication can be effective as it is fairly straightforward to implement and is easy to be accepted by the regulated user community.

→ There should be a method of ensuring that users do not share identification or authentication details (e.g. consider making it a violation of employment contract terms).

→ There should be a process for issuing new or changed passwords that:

a) ensures that passwords are not sent in the form of clear text e-mail messages

b) directly involves the person to whom the password uniquely applies

c) verifies the identity of the target user, such as via a special code or through independent confirmation

d) includes notification to users that passwords will expire soon.

→ Users' access rights should be:

a) restricted according to a defined policy, such as on a 'need to know' or 'need to restrict' basis

b) restricted according to users' individual roles

c) authorised by the application 'owner'

d) revoked promptly when an individual user is no longer entitled to them

e) enforced by automated access control mechanisms to ensure individual accountability.

→ Access to the application should be logged (see next section for further information).

As an important access control mechanism, users should be subjected to a rigorous sign-on process before they can gain access to the application. Sign-on mechanisms should be configured so that they:

a) display no identifying details until after sign-on is successful

b) warn that only authorized users are permitted access

c) validate sign-on information only when it has all been entered

d) limit the number of unsuccessful sign-on attempts

e) record all successful and unsuccessful sign-on attempts

f) restrict additional sign-on attempts

g) limit the duration of any one sign-on session

h) automatically re-invoke sign-on after an interruption of the process, for example when a connection is broken

i) advise users – on successful sign-on – of the date/time of their last successful sign-on and all unsuccessful sign-on attempts since their most recent successful sign-on

j) never store authentication details as clear text in automated routines

Security checklist

If you can satisfactorily answer the following questions, network security can be reasonably assured:

- Are access privileges to data files strictly controlled and users limited only to what they must access?

- Are access privileges to applications strictly controlled and users limited only to what they must access?

- Are users required to change passwords at predefined intervals?

- Are people with network admin authority required to change passwords at even more frequent intervals than users?

- After a predefined number of failed attempts, does an unsuccessful attempt result in suspension of the user's ID?

- Does a period of nonuse automatically log users off the network?

- Is user access limited to only the servers a user really needs to do his/her job?

Security checklist specific to EHR

- Does the system have time stamping performed on each entry for serving as audit trail?

- Does the system restrict access to certain system templates or features?

- Does the system have tracking feature that keeps track of which person documented what?

- Does the system enforce a strict security protocol and a practical "lock-out" feature?

- Does the system have adequate backup/recovery feature?

Establishing Accountability through event logging

Accountability determines who is responsible for a particular action taken. To properly establish accountability, audit trail and logging facility must be available. Your goal would be to address the following concerns:

- Do you maintain an audit trail of all additions, modifications and deletions to the network resources?

- Have you developed auditing and logging reports so potential problems can be identified and traced?

Logs should include sufficient information to provide a satisfactory audit trail. Additionally, they should be:

a) set to include all security-related events (you MUST always include the successful and failed access attempts)

b) reviewed periodically

c) retained for a specified period to comply with legal and regulatory requirements (7 years to be safe)

d) protected against unauthorized change.

Getting a little bit technical into computer security

The definition of the term network is that it is a group of computers, servers, workstations, mobile devices, printers, scanners, storage gears, and other devices that are connected together with cables or through wireless means. Information travels thus allowing network users to exchange data. Each computer, printer, scanner, device or other peripheral device that is connected is called a node. Network speed is expressed in megabits per second (or Mbps) and Gigabits per second (or Gbps). A network interface card (NIC, aka network adapter) is what is needed for network connection. A protocol is the basic language that both computers must use and follow in order to communicate. Computers generally send and receive data as packets. A protocol will work in various levels to modify, disassemble, and reassemble packets. All packets contain a number of specific information, including:

- source address

- destination address

- data transfer instructions

- reassembly method

- error checking information.

- actual data (aka payload)

A Network reference model is a blueprint for detailing the standards on how different protocols and products can communicate over the network. The OSI model is a network reference model with 7 layers. The Department of Defense DoD developed its own networking model known as the TCP/IP Model which has four layers. You can think of it as a consolidated 4-layer version of the 7-layer model.

A state of computer "security" is the conceptual ideal, attained by the use of the processes of Prevention, Detection, and Response.

Prevention:

User account access controls and cryptography can protect systems files and data, respectively. Firewalls are by far the most common prevention systems from a network security perspective as they can shield access to internal network services, and block certain kinds of attacks through packet filtering.

To prevent messages from being intercepted during transmission over the network, technologies like IPSec and SSL should be considered. They make it very time consuming to hack. Frankly, attackers love to attack a weak spot in a system than to touch a heavily fortified component. They are not likely to attack encrypted information communicated in a network because it would be VERY time consuming. Instead, the endpoints (e.g. the servers and the clients) are often the much easier targets.

Detection:

Intrusion Detection Systems are designed to detect network attacks in progress and assist in post-attack forensics, while audit trails and logs serve a similar function for individual systems.

Response:

"Response" is necessarily defined by the assessed security requirements of an individual system and may cover the range from simple upgrade of protections to notification of legal authorities, counter-attacks, and the like.

Defense in depth

A typical defense in depth approach divides the key security elements into layers for creating a cohesive defense strategy. To ensure effective IT security, you must design, implement, and manage IT security controls for each layer of this layered model. As an example: you may divide your controls into the layers of network, hardware, software, and data.

From a broader perspective, an important principle of the Defense in Depth strategy is that in order to achieve Information Assurance you need to maintain a balanced focus on the critical elements of People, Technology and Operations.

Security assumptions

In any case, security should not be view as an all or nothing issue. The designers and operators of systems should assume that security breaches are inevitable in the long term, that full audit trails should be kept of system activity so that when a security breach occurs, the mechanism and extent of the breach can be determined. In fact, storing audit trails remotely, where they can only be appended to, can keep intruders from covering their tracks.

A computer system is no more secure than the human systems responsible for its operation. Malicious individuals have regularly penetrated well-designed, secure computer systems by taking advantage of the carelessness of trusted individuals, or by deliberately deceiving them. The availability of the internet makes penetration even easier as everything is now connected.

Malware and Viruses

Malware is software designed to infiltrate or damage a computer system without the owner's informed consent. It is a blend of the words "malicious" and "software". The expression is a general term used by computer professionals to mean a variety of forms of hostile, intrusive, or annoying software or program code. Software is considered malware based on the intent of the creator rather than any particular features. It includes computer viruses, worms, trojan horses, spyware, adware, and other unwanted software.

The best-known types of malware are viruses and worms, which are known for the manner in which they spread, rather than any other particular behavior. Originally, the term computer virus was used for a program which infected other executable software, while a worm transmitted itself over a network to infect computers. More recently, the words are often used interchangeably.

Spyware applications are typically bundled as a hidden component of freeware or shareware programs that can be downloaded from the Internet. Once installed, the spyware monitors user activity on the Internet and transmits that information in the background to someone else. Since spyware is using memory and system resources for its own purpose at the background, it can lead to system crashes or general system instability.

As a common type of Trojan horses, a legitimate software might have been corrupted with malicious code which runs when the program is used. The key is that the user has to invoke the program in order to trigger the malicious code. In other words, a trojan horse simply cannot operate autonomously. You would also want to know that most but not all trojan horse payloads are harmful - a few of them are harmless. Most trojan horse programs are spread through e-mails. Some earlier trojan horse programs were bundled in "Root Kits". For example, the Linux Root Kit version 3 (lrk3) which was released in December 96 had tcp wrapper trojans included and enhanced in the kit.

Keystroke logging (in the form of spyware) was originally a function of diagnostic tool deployed by software developers for capturing user's keystrokes. This is done for determining the sources of error or for measuring staff productivity. Imagine if someone uses it to capture user input of critical business data such as CC info ... You may want to use anti spyware applications to detect and clean them up. Web-based on-screen keyboards may be a viable option for web applications. Keystroke Monitoring is a formal security process whereby administrators view and record the keystrokes entered by the user and the computer's immediate response. Keystroke Monitoring has to rely on keystroke logger to function though.

Identity theft occurs when someone uses another individual's personal information to take on that person's identity. This act could be much more than misuse of a name and a Social Security number as it often deals with fraudulent credit card use and mail fraud. Identity theft can become extremely easy when one's computer is being hacked into. That's why personal firewall should be used on desktop for home use.

Software Flaws

Computer code is regarded by some as just a form of mathematics. It is theoretically possible to prove the correctness of computer programs though the likelihood of actually achieving this in large-scale practical systems is regarded as unlikely in the extreme by most with practical experience in the industry.

In practice, only a small fraction of computer program code is mathematically proven, or even goes through comprehensive information technology audits or inexpensive but extremely valuable computer security audits.

Software flaws such as buffer overflows, are often exploited to gain control of a computer, or to cause it to operate in an unexpected manner. Buffer overflow (buffer overrun) is supposed to be a programming error which may result in memory access exception - that is, a process make attempt to store data beyond the fixed boundaries of a buffer area. With careless programming, this kind of access attempt can be triggered by ill-intended codes.

Stack-based buffer overflows and heap-based buffer overflows are the 2 popular types of attack of this nature. Techniques such as Static code analysis can help preventing such attack. You should also always opt for the use of safe libraries.

Many development methodologies rely on testing to ensure the quality of any code released; this process often fails to discover extremely unusual potential exploits. The term "exploit" generally refers to small programs designed to take advantage of a software flaw that has been discovered, either remote or local.

Sniffing, Eavesdropping, Footprinting and Social Engineering

As a pre-attack activity, footprinting refers to the technique of collecting information about systems thru techniques such as Ping Sweeps, TCP Scans, OS Identification, Domain Queries and DNS Interrogation. Passive fingerprinting, on the other hand, is based primarily on sniffer traces from your remote system. Rather than proactively querying a remote system, you capture packets that pass-by instead. Passive fingerprinting is very difficult to detect.

Any data that is transmitted over an IP network is at some risk of being eavesdropped or even modified.

Social engineering is a collection of techniques used to manipulate people into performing actions or divulging confidential information. While similar to a confidence trick or simple fraud, the term typically applies to trickery for information gathering or computer system access. Technically speaking, all Social Engineering techniques are based on flaws in human logic known as cognitive biases. These bias flaws are used in various combinations to create attack techniques. For example, pretexting is the act of creating and using an invented scenario (the pretext) to persuade a target to release information or perform an action and is usually done over the telephone. It's more than a simple lie as it most often involves some prior research or set up and the use of pieces of known information to establish legitimacy in the mind of the target.

Phishing, on the other hand, applies to email appearing to come from a legitimate business requesting "verification" of information and warning of some dire consequence if it is not done. Sadly, social engineering and direct computer access attacks can only be effectively prevented by non-computer means, which can be difficult to enforce, relative to the sensitivity of the information. Social engineering attacks in particular are very difficult to foresee and prevent.

Security management activities

The six major activities involved in information security management as according to the International Guidelines for Managing Risk of Information and communications Statement #1 (which was issued by the International Federation of Accountants) are:

- Policy Development— use the security objective and core principles as a framework around which to develop the security policy. You cannot afford to ignore the importance of policies. As a matter of fact, the MOST important responsibility of an information security manager in an organization is recommending and monitoring security policies.

- Roles and Responsibilities—ensure that individual roles, responsibilities and authority are clearly communicated and understood by all.

- Design—design and develop a security and control framework that consists of standards, measures, practices and procedures.

- Implementation—implement and maintain the solution on a timely basis,.

- Monitoring—establish monitoring measures to detect and ensure correction of security breaches, such that all actual and suspected breaches are promptly identified, investigated and acted upon, and to ensure ongoing compliance with policy, standards and minimum acceptable security practices.

- Awareness, Training and Education—create awareness of the need to protect information, providing training in the skills needed to operate information systems securely, and offering education in security measures and practices. **Training and awareness are vital in the overall strategy as security is often weakest at the end-user stage**.

Information Security Standards

The Federal Information Security Management Act (FISMA) is a US federal law enacted way back in 2002. It imposes a mandatory set of processes that have to be followed for information systems operated by a government agency or by a contractor which works on behalf of the agency. The Federal Information Processing Standards (FIPS), on the other hand, are a set of publicly announced standards developed by the US government for use by non-military government agencies and their contractors. FIPS 46 in particular covers some major Data Encryption Standards, while FIPS 140 covers security requirements for cryptography modules.

ISO 27001 sets out the requirements for information security management systems. On the other hand, ISO 27002 offers a code of practice for information security management.

British Standard 7799 Part 3 provides guidelines for information security risk management. COBIT links IT initiatives to business requirements, organises IT activities into a generally accepted process model, identifies the major IT resources to be leveraged and defines the management control objectives to be considered. ITIL (or ISO/IEC 20000 series) focuses on the service processes of IT and considers the central role of the user.

Trusted Computer System Evaluation Criteria (TCSEC) has classification on the various security requirements based on the evaluation of functionality, effectiveness and assurance of operating systems for the government and military sectors. TCSEC was introduced in 1985 and retired in 2000.

Information Technology Security Evaluation Criteria (ITSEC) is the first single standard for evaluating security attributes of computer systems by the countries in

Europe. Common Criteria (also known as ISO/IEC 15408) combines and aligns existing and emerging evaluation criteria with a collaborative effort among national security standards organizations of Canada, France, Germany, Japan, Netherlands, Spain, UK and US. Common Criteria Evaluation and Validation Scheme (CCEVS) establishes a national program for the evaluation of information technology products for conformance to the International Common Criteria for Information Technology Security Evaluation.

ISO/IEC 13335 (IT Security Management) offers a series of guidelines for technical security control measures. On the other hand, the Payment Card Industry Data Security Standard offers 12 core security requirements, which include security management, policies, procedures, network architecture, software design and other critical measures.

Control Objectives for Information and Related Technology (COBIT) was developed by ISACA as an accepted standard for IT security and control practices. It is intended for use by management, auditors, and security practitioners. It defines what has to be done for implementing an effective control structure.

EHR Upgrade

Before any system upgrade, one must formally review and verify the possible effects on EHR use and patient information. It is very important to test any EHR upgrades within an isolated test environment prior to applying the upgrade formally in a production environment.

One should develop a plan for the transition to the new EHR version. The plan must address the technical and organizational use of the new system. All training and procedure documents must be updated to account for the new version. And there must be adequate training to all users.

EHR Continuity and Disaster Recovery

BUSINESS CONTINUITY PLANNING (BCP) is the process of developing and documenting policies, procedures, and activities that can enable an organization to make proper response to an event that may last for an unacceptable or unexpectable period of time and then return to performing its critical business functions after such interruption. The resulting plan (the BUSINESS CONTINUITY PLAN) is the documentation you can rely on for purpose of ensuring business continuity.

Critical business functions are those that if interrupted or unavailable for several business days will significantly jeopardizing the operations of the organization. Each of these functions must be identified and given a priority classification as to its criticality to the overall business operation.

EHR must be treated as a critical business function and must be covered by the continuity planning process!

Recovery Time Objective (RTO) is defined as the time frame between an unplanned interruption of business operations and the resumption of business at a reduced level of service, while Recovery Point Objective (RPO) defines how much work in progress can be lost.

Generally speaking, the goals of RTO and RPO are not tightly coupled, nor are they completely decoupled. They should be determined independently, although it may be determined at some later point that they are interrelated due to infrastructure or technology issues.

Your BCP must address site selection and relocation for short-, medium-, and long-term disaster and disruption scenarios. Assuming a short term nature would be unrealistic. The goal here is to eliminate single-points-of-failure. Resiliency is the keyword. Below shows examples of backup sites (secondary sites). If you have the budget, you should get yourself at least one. If you don't have the budget, make the case to get this budget available.

Planning for recovery facilities must take into consideration factors such as location, size, capacity, as well as the required amenities necessary for recovering the level of service that is required by the critical business functions. When a major disaster is foreseeable, the BCP team should direct those business units with recovery processes to start preparing early in the alternate site. With enough preparation the business units can have ample time to test things out and make sure everything is operating correctly before the disaster is here.

Secondary sites (or backup sites) may come from several different sources, including commercial entities specializing in providing disaster recovery services <most expensive>; other locations you own; or a mutual agreement with another organization to share facilities <least expensive, but not easy to reach true agreement>

A hot site is a commercial disaster recovery service that allows a business to continue computer and network operations in the event of a computer or equipment disaster. A hot site provides all the equipment needed for the enterprise to continue operation, including office space and furniture, telephone jacks, and computer equipment...etc. **MOST EXPENSIVE TO KEEP, BUT HIGHLY EFFECTIVE.**

A hot site should be made sufficient in serving as a functional duplicate of a company's primary business location. There should be Capacity Management processes in place to ensure that adequate capacity is available at all times to meet the business requirements. There should also be Availability Management processes running to ensure that services at the hot site would meet or exceed their availability targets.

A cold site is a similar type of disaster recovery service that provides office space, but the customer provides and installs all the equipment needed to continue operations. It is less expensive, but it takes longer to get back to full operation after the disaster. **THE CHEAPEST TO KEEP.**

A warm site is stocked with hardware representing a reasonable facsimile of that found in your primary site. To restore service, you need to perform data restoration before recovery can begin. **A BALANCED OPTION BETWEEN COST AND EFFECTIVENESS.**

Synchronous Data Replication or mirroring refers to the process of copying data from one source to another in which an acknowledgement of the receipt of data at the copy location will be required in order for application processing to continue. Asynchronous Data Replication does not require acknowledgement of any kind. Electronic Vaulting refers to the back-up procedure of copying changed files and transmitting them to an off-site location via a batch process.

Typically, you can have an annual contract with a company that offers hot and cold site services with a monthly service charge schedule. A SLA may be one preferable option. Service Level Agreement (SLA) refers to that part of a service contract in which a certain level of service is agreed by the parties involved. A SLA is therefore NOT a type of service contract, but a part of a service contract. A contract containing SLA's is usually referred to, in legal terms, as a performance contract. Note that you don't want your hot/cold site to be located near your facility – some larger scale disasters like earthquake and flood can cause problem for the whole city!

Review Questions and Answers

1. What is health record?

2. A health record is derived from:

3. In the context of Medical-legal, what is the main use of the record?

4. A health record must contain sufficient information to:

5. How many health record should be kept for each patient?

6. In a source oriented medical record, the information about a patient's care and illness is typically organized according to:

7. What is flow sheet for?

8. Flow sheets are often used with what kind of health record?

9. Progress notes are in what format?

10. Healthcare location and setting information is typically captured by:

11. What is the most common form of database used in the healthcare industry?

12. What is a data warehouse?

13. What is the key to developing a quality health information database?

14. What is the foundation of every health database system?

15. A master table has a list of variables that represent:

16. What refers to one or more data attributes that uniquely identify an entity?

17. In the US, what is often being considered for use as the choice of patient identifier?

18. The Health Care Financing Administration (HCFA) has produced a popular provider identifier known as:

19. The Health Industry Number (HIN) was issued by the Health Industry Business Communications Council (HIBCC) to serve as:

20. The Labeler Identification Code (LIC) is issued by HIBCC for identifying:

21. The Universal Product Code (UPC) is maintained by the Uniform Code Council for:

22. The responsibility for the accuracy and completeness of a health record rests with:

23. What play a strategic role in providing access to computerized health information?

24. Standard vocabularies are a means of:

25. The Joint Commission on the Accreditation of Healthcare Organizations (JCAHO) sets standards for:

26. The Healthcare Information and Management Systems Society (HIMSS) is a membership organization which focuses on advocating:

27. What is Medicare?

28. Medicare has how many parts?

29. What is TRICARE?

30. Primary care describes:

31. Secondary care refers to:

32. Tertiary care refers to:

33. Quaternary care is an extension of:

34. Define Electronic Health Record.

35. The ASTM Standard _____ outlines practice for Content and Structure of the EHR.

36. _____ is a specific kind of digital medical record intended to be easily transported.

37. Compare EMRs with EHRs.

38. What is Clinical data repository?

39. What is HL7 for?

40. What is the preeminent healthcare IT standards developing organization in Europe?

41. FIPS 46 covers:

42. FIPS 140 covers:

43. ISO 27001 sets out the requirements for:

44. Accountability determines:

45. To properly establish accountability, what must be made available?

46. HIE focuses on:

Answers:

1. Formally speaking, a health record is a written collection of information about a patient.

2. A health record is derived from the patient's first encounter or treatment at a hospital, clinic or other primary health care centre.

3. In the context of Medical-legal, the main use of the record is as evidence of unbiased opinion of a patient's condition, history and prognosis, all assessed at a time when there was no thought of court action, and therefore extremely valuable.

4. A health record must contain sufficient information to IDENTIFY the patient, SUPPORT the diagnosis, JUSTIFY the treatment, and DOCUMENT the results facts accurately.

5. Only one health record should be kept for each patient.

6. In a source oriented medical record, the information about a patient's care and illness is typically organized according to the "source" of the information within the record, usually presented in chronological order.

7. Flow sheets provide the most appropriate method of monitoring a patient's progress.

8. Flow sheets are often used with source oriented health records.

9. Progress notes may be narrative or in the form of a flow sheet.

10. Healthcare location and setting information is typically captured by using specific synopsis data sets pre-established for each setting.

11. The most common form of database used in the healthcare industry is the relational database.

12. A data warehouse refers to a centrally managed yet easily accessible repository of data collected in the transaction information system. The data are usually aggregated, organized, catalogued and structured to facilitate read intensive search, queries, and analysis.

13. Data integrity is the key to developing a quality health information database. Without accurate data, the users will lose confidence in the database.

14. The foundation of every health database system is a database component called table.

15. A master table has a list of variables that represent the range of attributes currently defined for a given subject.

16. A primary key (PK) refers to one or more data attributes that uniquely identify an entity.

17. In the US, the Social Security Number (SSN) is often being considered for use as the choice of patient identifier.

18. The Health Care Financing Administration (HCFA) has produced a popular provider identifier known as the Universal Physician Identifier Number (UPIN), which can only be assigned to those physicians who handle Medicare patients.

19. The Health Industry Number (HIN) was issued by the Health Industry Business Communications Council (HIBCC) to serve as an identifier for healthcare facilities, practitioners, and retail pharmacies.

20. The Labeler Identification Code (LIC) is issued by HIBCC for identifying manufacturer and/or distributor.

21. The Universal Product Code (UPC) is maintained by the Uniform Code Council for labeling those products sold in retail channels.

22. The responsibility for the accuracy and completeness of a health record rests with the attending doctor.

23. Clinical Vocabularies play a strategic role in providing access to computerized health information since clinicians may use a variety of terms for the same concept.

24. Standard vocabularies are a means of encoding data for exchange, comparison, or aggregation among systems.

25. The Joint Commission on the Accreditation of Healthcare Organizations (JCAHO) sets standards for healthcare organizations and issues accreditation to organizations that meet those standards.

26. The Healthcare Information and Management Systems Society (HIMSS) is a membership organization which focuses on advocating the optimal use of healthcare information technology and management systems for the betterment of healthcare.

27. Medicare is a Federal health insurance program. It pays for hospital and medical care for the elderly (and also certain disabled Americans).

28. Medicare has two main parts for hospital and medical insurance (which are Part A and Part B) as well as two additional parts for flexibility and prescription drugs (which are Part C and Part D).

29. TRICARE is a health care program of the Department of Defense Military Health System which provides civilian health benefits for military personnel, military retirees, and their dependents.

30. Primary care describes the health services by those healthcare providers who server as the principal point of consultation for patients.

31. Secondary care refers to services provided by medical specialists who do not have first contact with patients.

32. Tertiary care refers to specialized consultative health care in facility that has personnel and equipments for advanced medical investigation and treatment.

33. Quaternary care is an extension of tertiary care in reference to highly specialized medicine of an advanced level. The services involved are usually only offered in a limited number of health care centers.

34. Electronic Health Record (EHR) is a longitudinal electronic record of patient health information generated by one or more encounters in any care delivery setting.

35. The ASTM Standard E1384 outlines practice for Content and Structure of the EHR.

36. Ambulatory EHR is a specific kind of digital medical record intended to be easily transported.

37. EMRs are computerized legal clinical records, while EHRs represent the ability to share medical information among stakeholders, including consumers, healthcare providers, employers and the government.

38. Clinical data repository (CDR) is a real-time transaction-processing database of all clinical patient information.

39. HL7 operates in the US for developing the most widely used healthcare-related electronic data exchange standards in North America.

40. CEN TC 215 is the preeminent healthcare IT standards developing organization in Europe.

41. FIPS 46 in particular covers some major Data Encryption Standards.

42. FIPS 140 covers security requirements for cryptography modules.

43. ISO 27001 sets out the requirements for information security management systems.

44. Accountability determines who is responsible for a particular action taken.

45. To properly establish accountability, audit trail and logging facility must be available.

46. Health information exchange HIE focuses on the mobilization of healthcare information electronically across organizations that use disparate health care information systems.

End of Book

Made in the USA
San Bernardino, CA
27 September 2015